W9-CPM-594

WITHDRAWN

Donated to
SAINT PAUL PUBLIC LIBRARY

Read All About
Horses

APPALOOSAS

LYNN M. STONE

The Rourke Corporation, Inc.
Vero Beach, Florida 32964

© 1998 The Rourke Corporation, Inc.

All rights reserved. No part of this book may be reproduced or utilized in any form or by any means, electronic or mechanical including photocopying, recording, or by any information storage and retrieval system without permission in writing from the publisher.

PHOTO CREDITS:
© Lynn M. Stone: cover, pages 4, 6, 7, 9, 15, 16, 18, 22; courtesy Appaloosa Journal: pages 10, 12, 13, 19, 21

EDITORIAL SERVICES:
Penworthy Learning Systems

Library of Congress Cataloging-in-Publication Data

Stone, Lynn M.
   Appaloosas / Lynn M. Stone.
     p. cm. — (Horses)
   Includes index.
   Summary: Describes the history and physical appearance of the spotted horses that were prized by the Nez Perce and have become a very popular breed in the United States today.
    ISBN 0-86593-510-6
   1. Appaloosa horse—Juvenile literature. [1. Appaloosa horse. 2. Horses.]
I. Title II. Series: Stone, Lynn M. Horses.
SF293.A7S86 1998
636.1'3—dc21
                                   98–25101
                                         CIP
                                         AC

Printed in the USA

TABLE OF CONTENTS

THE APPALOOSA

The Appaloosa is the Dalmatian of the horse world. Most Appaloosas, like Dalmatian dogs, have spots.

The Appaloosa is a true American **breed** (BREED) of riding horse. This breed, or type, of horse was first used by the Nez Percé (NAY per SAY) people of the Northwest.

Settlers called the spotted Nez Percé horses "Palouses." The Palouse River ran through Nez Percé territory. Later, the horses were called "Appalooseys." In 1938, the new Appaloosa Horse Club made "Appaloosa" the official name.

Once the pony of only the Nez Percé, the Appaloosa has become a favorite American breed.

THE FIRST SPOTTED HORSES

Spotted horses have always been popular. They even appeared on the walls of caves in France 20,000 years ago.

Between 2,500 and 3,500 years ago, artists in Egypt, Greece, Italy, and Austria painted spotted horses.

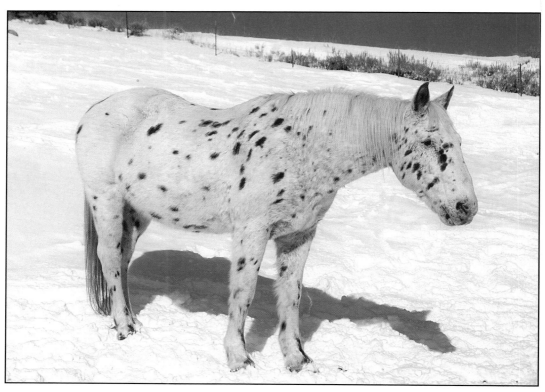

The Appaloosa's spots remind some of a Dalmatian's coat.

This Appaloosa has a white "blanket" with black spots.

Spotted horses were brought to China about 2,100 years ago. The Chinese loved them too, and many appeared in Chinese art.

The most recent **ancestors** (AN ses terz) of the Appaloosas, though, were spotted horses from Spain.

THE FIRST APPALOOSAS

Spanish explorers brought the spotted horses to North America about 500 years ago. By the 1700s, most Native American tribes in the West had horses. The Nez Percé were very choosy about their horses. They liked spotted horses, and they kept only the best.

Nez Percé horses—the first Appaloosas—were fast, intelligent, and tireless. The spots made the horses beautiful, but they also helped hide the animals in the shadows.

Good "horse sense" helped make the Appaloosa a favorite among the Nez Percé.

THE HISTORY OF THE APPALOOSA

Like the Nez Percé themselves, other Western tribes loved the Nez Percé horses. But the U.S. Army felt differently.

In 1877, army horsemen captured the last of the Nez Percé men, women, and children. The capture ended a war between the army and the Nez Percé.

The soldiers feared that the Nez Percé might escape on their horses. To prevent that, the soldiers killed most of the Nez Percé horses. A few horses escaped.

The army kept a few horses, but foolishly mated them with their heavy work horses.

Prince Charles would never have been aboard a polo-playing Appaloosa had not the breed been rescued from extinction in the late 1800s.

THE APPALOOSA IN AMERICA

Almost overnight, the beautiful Nez Percé Appaloosa was nearly wiped out. Fortunately, a few horse **breeders** (BREE derz) located and saved some of the last Appaloosas.

One reason for the Appaloosa's popularity is its ability to do many things well, including work as a cow horse.

An Appaloosa mount is a familiar sight in the western U.S.A.

The comeback of the Appaloosa was slow. There were only 200 **registered** (REJ iss terd) Appaloosas in 1947.

Today, the Appaloosa Horse Club lists more than 500,000 registered Appaloosas. The breed has become one of the most popular in the world, especially in the United States.

THE APPALOOSA BODY

Horse breeders are concerned about the way a horse is built. Each breed has certain features. Those features help set one breed apart from others. Breeders call an animal's overall build its **conformation** (kon for MAY shun).

In the Appaloosa, the head is small and the nose is straight. The App has pointed ears, large eyes, and a long, muscular neck. It has a deep chest and solid legs.

The Appaloosa stands 14 to 16 **hands** (HANDZ) at its shoulders. Each hand is four inches (ten centimeters).

Pointed ears and the trademark spots are among the Appaloosa's markers.

THE APPALOOSA COAT

Most Appaloosas are spotted, especially on their hips. Some Appaloosas have spots on spots! Some have roan coloring. Roan animals have light hairs scattered against a darker background.

Appaloosa breeders describe the breed's color patterns as snowflake, leopard, marble, frost, spotted blanket, and white blanket.

Don't confuse horses with large blotches of brown and white or black and white with Appaloosas. These horses are most likely pintos, or "paints."

A pinto wears large blotches of white, rather than spots or flecks.

GROWING UP AN APPALOOSA

Appaloosa babies, like those of other horses, are called **foals** (FOLZ). An Appaloosa foal develops in its mother, a **mare** (MAIR), for 11 months. At birth, the foal weighs more than 100 pounds (45 kilograms).

An Appaloosa foal nuzzles its mother.

Ready for riding, a young Appaloosa on lead awaits a saddle.

The foal nurses on mother's milk for about five months. Meanwhile, it begins to eat solid foods too, like grass and grain.

By age two or three, a young horse is ready for training as a riding animal.

APPALOOSAS AT WORK

Appaloosas are used for many different types of riding. Some are used for middle-distance racing. Others are used in the demanding riding events of a style called **dressage** (dreh SAHJH).

Cowboys use Appaloosas as roping horses. Appaloosas are used as jumpers and for trail riding. Both children and adults can feel comfortable on the even-tempered Appaloosas.

Like the original Nez Percé Appaloosas, some modern Apps are prized for their ability to stay strong. These Appaloosas are ridden up to 100 miles (160 kilometers) per day in distance contests!

An Appaloosa races around barrels in competition.

GLOSSARY

ancestors (AN ses terz) — those of the same family who came before

breed (BREED) — a particular group of domestic animals having the same characteristics, such as shape or color

breeder (BREE der) — one who raises animals, such as horses, and lets them reproduce

conformation (kon for MAY shun) — the body build of a domestic animal

dressage (dreh SAHJH) — complex moves by a horse in response to a rider's shifting weight

foal (FOL) — a horse before the age of one year

hand (HAND) — a four-inch (ten-centimeter) measure of horses' shoulder height

mare (MAIR) — a mother horse

registered (REJ iss terd) — listed officially in a book (register) as part of a specific breed

An Appaloosa (left) uses its front feet to clear snow from buried grass in a Colorado blizzard.

INDEX

FURTHER READING

Find out more about horses with these helpful books and organization:

Clutton-Brock, Juliet. *Horse.* Knopf, 1992.

Edwards, Elwyn H. *The Encyclopedia of the Horse.* Dorling Kindersley, Inc., 1994.

Hendricks, Bonnie. *International Encyclopedia of Horse Breeds.* University of Oklahoma, 1995.

Appaloosa Horse Club, 5070 Highway 8 West, Moscow, ID 83843, or online at http://www.appaloosa.com

1— 6/01